Cannibal Animals

Cannibal Animals

Animals That Eat Their Own Kind

Anthony D. Fredericks

Franklin Watts
A Division of Grolier Publishing
New York • London • Hong Kong • Sydney
Danbury, Connecticut

To Brad Rehnberg,
who continues to respond to my never-ending barrage
of questions with good humor and insightful erudition.

Note to readers: Definitions for words in **bold** can be found in the Glossary at the back of this book.

Photographs ©: Gamma-Liaison: 8, 9 (G. Brad Lewis), 11 (Sam Sargent), 48; Photo Researchers: 16 (Fletcher & Baylis), cover (Tim Davis), 30, 31 (Dan Guravich), 29 (Clem Haagner), 25, 32, 44, 46 (Tom & Pat Leeson), 45 (Jeff Lepore), 34, 35 (Maslowski), 22 (Van Nostrand), 5 left, 19, 52 (Len Rue Jr.), 36, 37 (Helen Williams); Visuals Unlimited: 1 (Gerald & Buff Corsi), 14 (Beth Davidow), 20, 43 (Elizabeth DeLaney), 49, 50 (Ken Lucas), 28 (S. Maslowski), 6 (Steve McCutcheon), 17, 40, 42 (Joe McDonald), 38 (Ron Spomer), 5 right, 12, 13 (Tom Ulrich); Wildlife Collection: 10 (Bob Bennett).

Visit Franklin Watts on the Internet at:
http://publishing.grolier.com

Library of Congress Cataloging-in-Publication Data

Fredericks, Anthony D.
    Cannibal Animals: animals that eat their own kind / by Anthony D. Fredericks
       p.   cm.— (Watts Library)
    Includes bibliographical references and index.
    Summary: Describes the reasons for and instances of cannibalistic behavior in a variety of animals, including guppies, black widow spiders, sharks, gerbils, and brown bears.
    ISBN 0-531-11701-4 (lib. bdg.)   0-531-16420-9 (pbk.)
    1. Cannibalism in animals—Juvenile literature. [1. Cannibalism in animals. 2. Animals—Habits and behavior.] I. Title. II. Series
QL756.57.F74   1999
591.5'3—dc21   98-30030
                                                                  CIP
                                                                  AC

Contents

A modern-day headhunter with a "trophy"

Chapter One

Why Be a Cannibal?

Have you ever heard stories about cannibals—people in distant lands who eat other human beings for dinner? These stories may give you the creeps, and you may even wonder if cannibals really exist. Are cannibals for real? The answer is yes, they are! In the animal world, **cannibalism**, killing and eating members of an animal's own species, or kind, happens every day.

Why are animals cannibals? One basic reason is survival. For you and me, survival means staying alive. It also means eating nutritious food, getting enough sleep, and following basic rules of safety. For example, we wear bicycle helmets, stay away from tall trees during lightning storms, and use seat belts. In the animal world, however, survival has a different meaning.

The survival of an animal species isn't just about how an animal lives or dies. It is also about the species' ability to give birth to a new generation. The survival of a species depends mainly on how well it adapts to a changing environment. Those changes may include changes in climate, in plant life, and in the types and numbers of predators and **prey**.

Scientists believe that, over time, animals develop special traits and behaviors that help them survive to produce another generation. This process, known as **evolution**, takes place over many thousands of years. Species that don't change, or evolve, die out and become **extinct**.

One major question in the ability of an animal species to survive is: How does it get its food? Biologists have estimated that there are more than 1,300 kinds of cannibal animals— species that eat members of their own kind. While we may think that cannibalism is gross, it's important to remember that it is a normal and natural part of the lives of many creatures.

Heads Up!

A female praying mantis rests quietly on the branch of a tall oak tree. She is waiting for an unsuspecting insect to come near enough to capture. A male praying mantis approaches

A female praying mantis gets ready for dinner.

silently from the rear. It is autumn, the time when males and females mate.

The male praying mantis is much smaller than the female, so he must be careful as he approaches her. Suddenly, he leaps on the back of the female and begins to mate with her. During this process, the female may turn her head and bite off the head of the male. Amazingly, the mating process continues between the female and her headless companion. Afterward, it is not unusual for the female to completely devour the male. Then, before the chill of winter sets in, the female lays her eggs.

Jaws of Death

A praying mantis captures a victim with its front legs. The legs snap shut like a pair of pliers and hold the prey with sharp hooks. The mantis begins to eat the helpless victim while it is still alive.

A praying mantis rests after her deadly meal.

It may be hard to imagine, but this happens all the time. Praying mantises, or **mantids,** spend most of the summer catching spiders and insects. As their bodies become larger, they shed their hard outer covering or **exoskeleton**. About 2 weeks after the last molting, the males are ready to mate.

Unfortunately, the mating process often results in the male becoming dinner for the female. While this may seem cruel to us it serves an important function for these creatures. The female needs lots of energy to produce her eggs. She gets a good meal in late autumn when insect food may be scarce.

Brotherly Love?

When the young mantids emerge from the eggs in the spring, they often eat one another. In other words, their first meal after birth may be their brothers and sisters.

Eat or Be Eaten!

There are several reasons for cannibalism in the animal kingdom. Interestingly, scientists often have difficulty separating one reason from another. That's because, in some cases, several factors may be working together to stimulate cannibalism in a species.

Exploitation of Same Species

For many animals, cannibalism is beneficial because it provides food quickly and easily. Most animals produce more young than can possibly survive. In this situation, some animals exploit, or take advantage of, weaker animals. As a result, crowded conditions provide food for the strongest individuals.

Elimination of Competitors

Another benefit of cannibalism is that it gets rivals for food out of the picture. In many ecosystems, there is enormous competition for food. By eating members of its own kind, especially younger and smaller individuals, an animal is eliminating future competitors.

Population Control

In many species, too many offspring are produced and there may not be enough food to feed them all. In some years or some seasons food may be scarce. As a result, large numbers of animals may die off. By killing and eating their young, some species adapt their population to the amount of available food. This kind of population control is quite common throughout the animal world.

Cannibalism in the animal world may be more common than you think. It is probably going on right now—in your backyard, just down the street, or in the branches of a nearby tree. It's important to remember that this is how some species of animals have been able to survive for thousands of years.

From High to Low

Scientists recognize two forms of cannibalism. "High grade" or frequent cannibalism may be harmful to a species. If too many members of a species are killed, the species may become extinct.

"Low grade" or infrequent cannibalism may be beneficial. For example, if two members of the same species fight, the weaker member dies and becomes food for the stronger member. That means that the stronger member survives, reproduces, and is able to produce another generation.

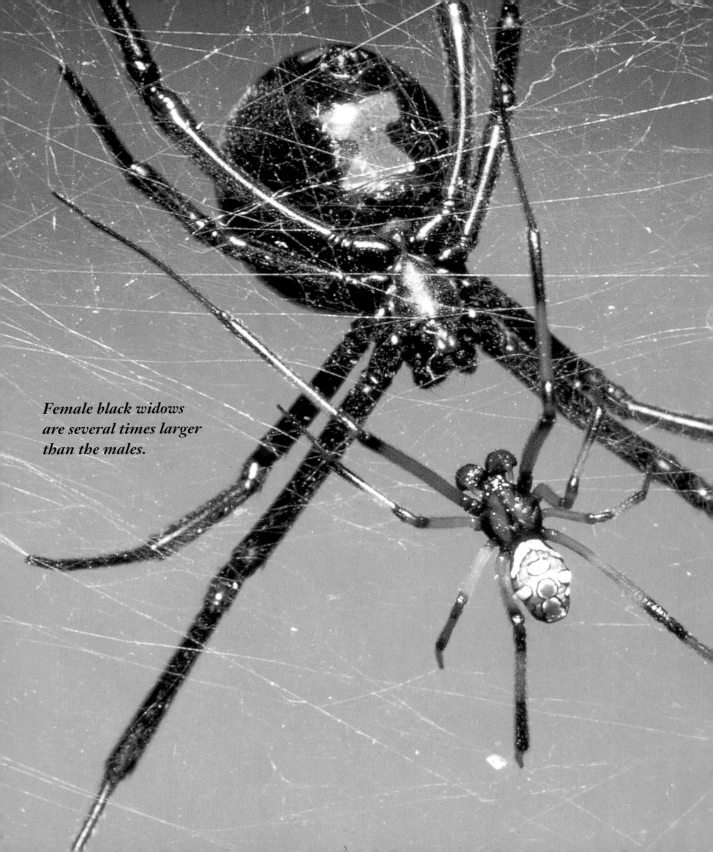

Female black widows are several times larger than the males.

Chapter Two

Tiny Cannibals

When we think of cannibal animals, we may think of creatures with enormous teeth and massive bodies. But cannibals come in all shapes and sizes. Indeed, some of the most dangerous animals—at least to their own kind—may be some of the smallest.

Black widow spiders are among the most well-known creatures in the animal kingdom. However, their reputation as dangerous critters does not match their small size. Scary stories surround this

A black widow with its distinctive hourglass pattern

tiny spider—turning it into a creature that is often larger than life.

These spiders can be found in the warmer parts of the world. Their most remarkable physical feature is the red hourglass shape on the underside of their bellies. Black widows build their webs in abandoned buildings, cellars, attics, and other cool dark places. There they wait for flies or other insects to fly into their webs and be trapped by the strands of silk.

Black widow spiders get their name from the fact that the female sometimes eats the male after mating. Many people believe that females always eat the males, but scientists have

Black widow spiders can be dangerous creatures, not only to the insects they capture and eat, but to humans as well. Although these spiders tend to avoid people, the bite of a female black widow spider is sometimes fatal to humans. In fact, the **venom** of a black widow is fifteen times more deadly than a rattlesnake's poison.

proved otherwise. Females eat their mates only if they are hungry. So the male black widow spider must play a guessing game, hoping that the female is not hungry when he approaches. This is even more dangerous because the female is always larger than the male.

All My Brothers and Sisters

Not only are black widow spiders cannibalistic during mating, but they are equally dangerous to one another right after hatching. After mating, the female black widow lays up to 1,000 eggs in an egg sac in the middle of her web. After a few days tiny **spiderlings** hatch and begin to scurry over the web.

Unfortunately, the spiderlings usually have nothing to eat but one another. Until they are old enough to build their own webs, larger

A female black widow guards her egg case.

15

spiderlings often eat their smaller brothers and sisters. Typically, less than 25 percent of newborn black widow spiders survive to adulthood.

Chewing Children

Midges are tiny insects found throughout North America and Europe. There are three families of these small mosquito-like flies: the non-biting midges, the biting midges (which are a summertime pest along the Atlantic seaboard and are often called "no-seeums"), and the gall midges, which do serious damage to crops.

Like many insects, midges go through a process known as **metamorphosis** in which they change from an egg into an adult. Butterflies and moths are examples of insects that begin their lives as caterpillars and, through metamorphosis, become beautiful winged creatures. Midges go through four stages of development—egg, **larva**, **pupa**, and adult. In all cases, the adults look completely different from the young.

Midges can infect plant leaves throughout the forest.

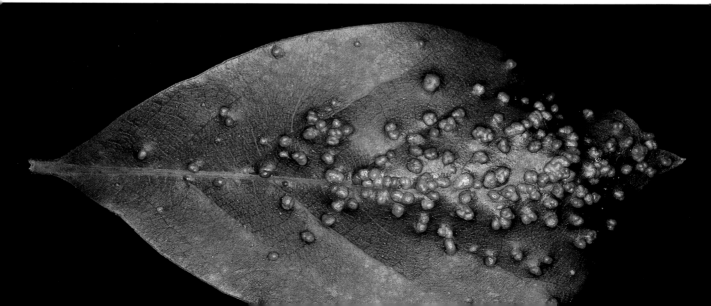

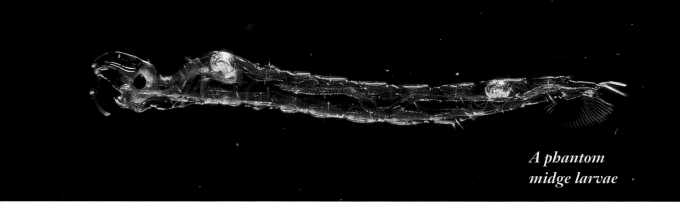

A phantom midge larvae

Yet, something very peculiar happens in some species of midges. Females develop eggs inside their bodies, but these eggs are not fertilized by a male. The females keep the eggs inside their bodies and the eggs develop into larvae. The one thing all larvae do is feed constantly, and these midge larvae are no different. The only difference is that they feed on their mother—from the inside out. Eventually they kill her and break free. This action may be repeated for several generations.

Entomologists, scientists who study insects, have learned that this behavior is often dependent upon the temperature. Cooler temperatures tend to stimulate this strange behavior, while warmer temperatures cause the midges to revert back to their normal four-stage cycle.

Free Meal!

One species of biting midge attacks mosquitoes and sucks the blood mosquitoes have sucked from other animals.

Watch Out for Mom and Dad!

Guppies are found around the islands of the southern Caribbean Sea. They are also one of the best-known and most popular home aquarium fish. The males are brightly colored in combinations of yellow, red, orange, green, blue, purple,

A colorful male and drab female guppy begin their courtship "dance."

and spots of black. Like the fingerprints of humans, no two males have exactly the same pattern. Female guppies, on the other hand, are quite drab.

The rich colors of the male are used to attract females during a fancy courtship dance. Males swim back and forth in front of the females showing off their colors and spreading their fins. Four weeks after mating, the female produces a group of young guppies called fry.

For reasons that are not entirely clear, the birth of their young turns the adults of some guppy species into cannibals.

Soon after the birth of the babies, the parents turn on their own young—attacking and eating them. The fry are more likely to be eaten when they are in open water, such as in an aquarium without plants. In the wild, baby guppies that hide in plants on the bottom are the most likely to survive.

The young guppies that escape from their parents are also the ones most likely to escape from any would-be predators. Strange as it may seem, the parents that eat their babies are doing a good thing. They are making sure that only the strongest of their species survive to produce future generations.

Alligators belong to a group of animals called reptiles.

Chapter Three

Reptilian and Amphibian Cannibals

Reptiles and amphibians are two of the most diverse groups of animals on Earth. There are more than 6,000 species of reptiles and more than 4,000 species of amphibians. Reptiles spend most of their lives on land, while amphibians live on land and in water. Examples of reptiles include snakes, turtles, alligators, and crocodiles. Amphibians include salamanders, frogs, and newts.

The First Cannibal Animal

When most people think of dinosaurs, they think of *Tyrannosaurus rex*—the most "famous" of all dinosaurs. *T. rex* was certainly the biggest and heaviest of all the meat-eating dinosaurs—reaching a length of 40 feet (12.2 meters), a height of 18 feet (5.5 m), and a body weight of nearly 7 tons.

T. rex lived about 65 million years ago in what are now the states of Montana, Wyoming, and South Dakota, as well as in the Canadian province of Alberta. During this time, the north-central part of the United States was a lush environment of forests and streams—an ideal location for plant-eaters and for the meat-eaters that fed on them.

Recently, scientists in South Dakota discovered three *Tyrannosaurus* skeletons that indicate that *T. rex* may have been a cannibal! One of the skeletons had a hole in the back of its skull matching the shape of a *T. rex* tooth. Another skeleton,

That's Really Big!

Here's another way to look at the size of a *Tyrannosaurus rex*: It was as long as two school buses in a row, as tall as a two-story house, and it weighed as much as 185 average fifth-graders.

Learning about dinosaurs is exciting, but takes hard work.

a female, had a 6-inch (15-cm)-long *T. rex* tooth embedded in a broken rib. And fatal wounds on the left side of the skull were the result of another *T. rex* bite. A third specimen had **vertebrae** (bones in the spine) that were bitten in half, along with several other bones that had been chewed out of its skeleton. *T. rex* seems to have lived up to its name— "tyrant-lizard king."

The scientists studying these skeletons think that *Tyrannosaurus rex* may have eaten its own kind. These creatures engaged in ferocious battles—often in defense of their territories. But these three skeletons indicate that *T. rex* might also have been cannibalistic. Research is still being conducted to determine why *Tyrannosaurus rex* might have

feasted on one another. Scientists believe it may have been because there were few, if any, other animals to attack. So *T. rex* could have turned on a member of its own group to get a quick and easy meal.

T. rex wasn't always a successful predator.

Eating Machine

You could say that the "diet" of a tiger salamander is like the diet of a typical teenager—anything and everything! Young tiger salamanders have huge appetites and will eat almost anything they can get into their mouths—ants, worms, snails, mice, or other small animals. If it moves, it's food for a tiger salamander.

Tiger salamanders are found in mountain forests, sagebrush plains, and damp meadows. Typically, they prefer to live close to a lake, stream, or temporary rain pool. Adults spend most of their time underground, emerging only to seek out a mate and breed. Young salamanders spend most of their time eating—sometimes each other.

Scientists have discovered that the young in some groups of tiger salamanders are cannibals. In these groups, cannibalism occurs most frequently when the salamanders live in very crowded conditions. The cannibalistic salamanders develop specialized structures in their mouths that help them eat other salamanders. Also, the larvae of cannibals tend to grow larger than the larvae of non-cannibals.

Cannibalism in tiger salamanders is a beneficial behavior because it accomplishes two things. It offers a quick and readily available food source and it eliminates competitors for other kinds of food. As cruel as that may seem to you and me, it has allowed this species to survive for thousands, perhaps millions, of years.

Bigger Than You!

The largest salamander in the world is the Chinese giant salamander. It grows up to 5 feet (1.5 m) long—that's longer than the average sixth-grader is tall—and weighs about 220 pounds (100 kilograms).

Salamanders
sometimes look like
snakes with legs.

Hopping Gulpers

A ferocious-looking creature, the horned frog gets it name from the two hornlike body parts that stick out over its eyes. These are not true horns, however. They are flaps of skin and are neither hard nor sharp. The horned frog, one of the largest members of the frog family, may grow up to 10 inches (25 cm) long. It has a broad head with a very wide mouth, so it is sometimes referred to as the wide-mouthed frog.

South American horned frogs live near rivers and swamps. They like to lie half buried in soft ground. They can hide easily because their body shape and coloring blend into the leaves and other plantlife on the ground. There, they wait for any likely prey, such as insects, lizards, snakes, small birds, and even small animals.

When they are hungry, horned frogs jump at anything that moves. If there are many horned frogs in a particular area, the

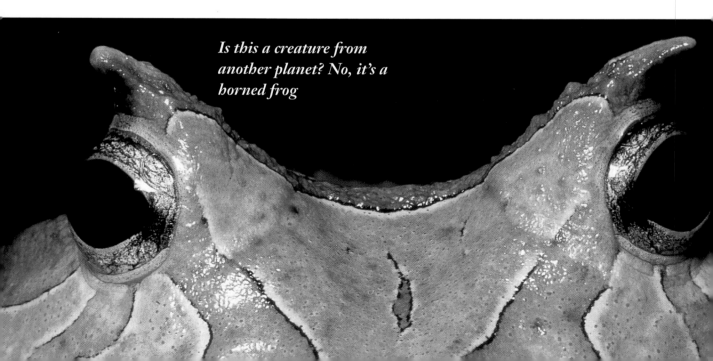

Is this a creature from another planet? No, it's a horned frog

This Argentine horned frog feasts on a rodent.

larger members will attack and devour the smaller members. Unfortunately, a horned frog is not very good at judging size, so it sometimes makes the mistake of attacking and attempting to swallow a larger frog. In such cases, one frog gets caught inside another frog's throat. Since frogs tend to swallow whatever they catch, this "stalemate" may last for several hours. In some cases, the frog trying to swallow will die. Unfortunately, the victim is still stuck in the mouth of the predator and it may die too.

Scientists think cannibalism among horned frogs is their way of controlling their numbers. Since these frogs have so few enemies, they reduce their population by eating one another.

Udderly Incredible

Some species of horned frogs make a croak that sounds just like the "Moo" of a cow.

29

The great white shark is able to detect one part blood in 10 million parts of sea water.

Chapter Four

Underwater Cannibals

Cannibalistic animals are found on almost every continent in the world. They live in the deepest jungles, the highest mountains, and the driest deserts. It should be no surprise, then, that cannibal animals are also found underwater. Some of the strangest and most unusual cannibal animals live in the oceans.

Books, articles, and movies describe sharks as vicious and deadly creatures. Tales of attacks by man-eating sharks flood our imaginations and fill the pages of newspapers and magazines around the world. Although there are fewer than thirty recorded shark attacks on humans each year, these creatures have acquired a killing reputation.

Unfortunately, this reputation has also helped place a number of shark species on the endangered species list. Sharks are sometimes hunted and killed simply because they are sharks. As a result, several species are on the verge of extinction.

However, one species of shark—the sand tiger shark—is a deadly and dangerous creature—not to humans, but to members of its own kind. It practices the most unusual form of cannibalism in the animal world—intrauterine cannibalism. The sand tiger shark eats its siblings before birth, while they are still inside their mother's body.

An Inside Job

After mating, a female sand tiger shark produces up to 100 fertilized eggs. These eggs develop and grow inside the female's two **oviducts**. Some eggs grow faster and develop more quickly than others. The first young in each oviduct to reach 2 1/2 inches (6 centimeters) in size tears open its egg within the mother's **uterus** and begins to feed on all the undeveloped eggs. It continues this feeding pattern until it is the only one left.

After a long **gestation** or period of growth inside the mother's body, the mother shark gives birth to one or two shark pups—each of which is about 3 feet (1 m) long. These pups are the only survivors of an initial group of dozens and

Great White Terror

Recent studies by scientists suggests that the best-known and most feared shark of all—the great white shark— may also practice a form of intrauterine cannibalism.

Some species of shark cannibalize their own eggs.

dozens of eggs. This unusual form of cannibalism, in which the young eat their brothers and sisters before birth, ensures that only the strongest sand tiger sharks are born.

Father Knows Best

In every species of animal, it is the female that produces eggs. However, eggs need to be fertilized by a male before they can grow and develop. In some species, the eggs develop inside the mother's body and the babies are born alive. In other species, the mother lays eggs that hatch outside her body. Most animal parents do not guard their eggs. As a result, many eggs never hatch, simply because they are discovered and eaten by other animals.

In several animal species, though, the eggs or young need constant attention in order to survive. Quite often, it is the female who hatches the eggs and takes care of the young during the early stages of their lives.

However, in a few species, it is the male that watches over the eggs or takes care of the young during their first few weeks of life. One such example is the damselfish, a small, sometimes brightly colored fish, that lives among the coral reefs and rocks of warm-water seas.

During the breeding season, the female damselfish lays large quantities of eggs—often up to 300,000—in and around submerged rocks. Then the female leaves, never to see her eggs again. The male, however, stays with the eggs—guarding them and **aerating** them, supplying them with oxygen by constantly moving its fins back and forth. Because there are so many eggs, the male is in constant motion—chasing off would-be predators while keeping

Male damselfish fiercy guard thousands of eggs— all at the same time.

the eggs properly aerated. The male does this until the eggs hatch.

With so many eggs to protect, male damselfish don't have many opportunities to eat. As a result, males often eat some of the eggs they are guarding. This reduces the number of eggs, but ensures that the others have a better chance for survival. In some cases, if the number of eggs is small, the male damselfish may eat most or all of the eggs in his care. In short, he cannibalizes the very eggs he is protecting.

Purple sea snails float upside down on homemade bubble rafts.

Just Float On By

The purple sea snail spends its entire life hanging upside down. It does this by creating its own small bubble raft. The sea snail secretes milky white bubbles or **froth** from its foot, which traps air into a collection of bubbles. The bubbles are coated with a special **mucus** that hardens into a jellylike substance. The snail glues all the bubbles together into a sort of raft from which it hangs upside down. The snail then spends its life floating on ocean currents or being carried on the wind.

At first glance, you may think this little creature is quite harmless—but don't tell that to a sea jelly! Purple sea snails just love to eat sea jellies. While they are floating, the snails can detect the presence of sea jellies through sense organs near their mouths. Although sea snails have no eyes, they are quite good at locating prey.

Sometimes it is difficult for sea snails to locate enough sea jellies, though. At such times, these creatures eat members of their own kind to survive.

When it locates a sea jelly or another purple sea snail, the sea snail releases a dye that makes its victim unable to move. The stunned victim is eaten by the snail until only a few floating remains are left. After feeding, the female sea snail may lay as many as 3 million tiny eggs on the underside of its dead victim.

The purple sea snail has adapted to its environment in a special way. Typically, seas snails live in large groups, floating together through tropical waters. However, like many other species of animals, their survival and reproduction depends on how well they are able to locate food—even if that food is one of their own kind.

Pet gerbils are fun to care for and observe.

Chapter Five

Furry Cannibals

With more than 1,300 different species of cannibal animals, it should not be surprising to discover that several are mammals—warm-blooded animals that nourish their young with milk. While we certainly wouldn't expect fierce cannibalistic behavior from our pet dog or cat, there are cannibal mammals. Some live in the wild, but others do not. You may have seen one at the zoo, in a pet store, in a circus, or at school—or one may even live at home with you.

Cuddly Cannibals

Gerbils are among the most popular small pets in the United States. But, did you know that they are also cannibalistic?

Of the ninety species of gerbils in the world, the Mongolian gerbil is the one most often kept as a pet. It was discovered in eastern Mongolia in 1897; however, it wasn't imported into the United States until 1954. In the wild, these gerbils normally live in large burrows that extend underground and have several chambers for nesting and storing food. Although they are primarily plant eaters, wild gerbils sometimes supplement their diet with a few insects—or other gerbils.

Baby gerbils are helpless when born.

Female gerbils give birth to several **litters** of young a year—with one to eight babies in each litter. The birth takes place about 3 weeks after mating and the babies stay with the mother for another 3 weeks. However, it is not unusual for a gerbil mother to attack and eat her own babies.

Cannibalistic behavior in female gerbils occurs when the mother does not get enough protein, an important nutrient, in her diet. The easiest way to get some extra protein is by eating her own babies. Sometimes babies are born dead or have birth defects. In such cases, the mother eats part, or all, of the bodies. As a result, the babies' protein and other nutrients are recycled back into the mother's body.

Overcrowding in a group of gerbils may lead to other forms of cannibalistic behavior. One form occurs when there is more than one mother in a nest at the same time. If one mother's litter is left unguarded, the young may be killed and eaten by the mother of another litter. Another form of cannibalism occurs when there is not enough food available. In those cases, a mother may kill and eat her new litter while protecting and defending an older litter.

While gerbils are a popular pet, it is important to keep some of their behaviors in mind. Sometimes, cannibalism in the females is stimulated when humans handle the babies. When that happens, the mother and her young must be separated.

A gerbil just six hours after birth

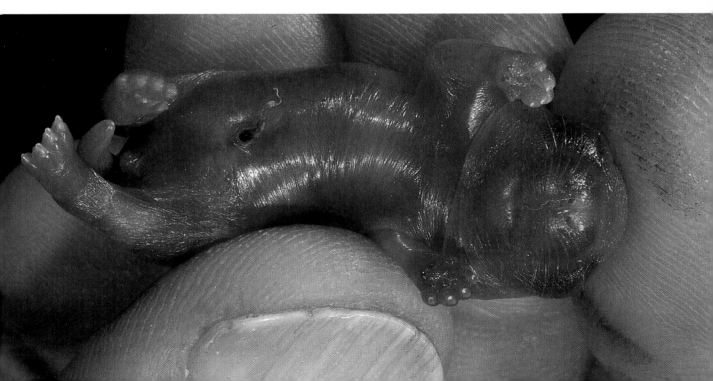

Big Bad Brown Bears

Brown bears are found in many parts of Canada and Alaska.

Alaskan brown bears, or Kodiak bears, live on the shores and islands of Alaska. Like other species of bears, they are solitary animals, except during the summer breeding season. At this time, these bears eat more than usual so they can store up fat for the winter.

The female brown bear gives birth to one or two cubs at a time—with a litter every 2 years. The cubs stay with their mother for the first year or two, and then begin to venture out on their own. During this part of their lives, they are most at risk of attack—particularly by adult males.

It is not unusual for males to attack and eat young cubs. This, of course, removes future competitors—for food as well as for mates. If food supplies are low in a particular area, the young cubs are readily available and easy to catch. Also, adult males do not want competition for the few breeding females in their territories. By killing and eating cubs—especially male cubs—the adult males ensure their control of a specific area.

Unfortunately, many of the natural habitats of brown bears throughout North America are being destroyed by human

Sleep It Off

Did you know that bears do not go into true **hibernation** in the winter? Instead, they enter a state known as "winter sleep." This allows them to wake up to care for their cubs or walk about on mild winter days.

carelessness. The growth of cities and farmland have reduced many bear populations—much more than cannibalism has.

Though powerful enough to kill humans, brown bears rarely attack them.

Treetop Terrors

Chimpanzees are among the most recognizable animals in the world, and have always been a favorite of zoo visitors. Wild chimps live in the rain forests of Africa. They make their nests in the trees and descend to the ground to search for food. They eat a variety of foods, and chimps are one of the few animals to use tools to gather food.

Deadlier than the Female

In several species of animals, cannibalism is part of the reproductive process. Male lions and barn cats sometimes kill and eat the cubs of another male. When this happens, the mothers of those cubs often become ready to mate again. This allows the killer males to mate with the mothers of the cubs they just ate. It is one way to ensure that only the strongest members of a species produce future generations.

Chimpanzees in a community relate to one another in complex ways. Male rule may depend on the age of a male, his ability to make noisy displays, or his tendency to run around waving branches in the air.

The ruling males in a troop sometimes kill and eat infants of new or low-ranking females—infants that are probably the offspring of another male. This ensures that the ruling male is protecting his own offspring in his troop. In short, ruling males practice cannibalism to protect their bloodlines and ensure that their own offspring will eventually be the rulers in a colony.

Although we may enjoy the antics of chimpanzees at the circus or zoo, it is interesting to think about how some of their behaviors mirror our own. Behaviors that ensure survival are common among chimpanzees, humans, and many other kinds of animals throughout the world.

A chimpanzee threatens an intruder with a stick.

Distant Relatives

Chimpanzees are the animals nearest in intelligence to human beings. They are more closely related to humans than any other animal.

Elaborate cannibalistic rituals took place at ancient Aztec temples like this one.

Chapter Six

Humans, Survival, and Cannibalism

Are you still wondering if humans can be cannibals? For centuries, stories of human cannibalism have come from Africa, the South Pacific, and even North and South America. Cannibalism has been—and may still be—practiced in some parts of the world. However, it is safe to say that many reports of cannibalism have been exaggerated simply for the sake of telling a grisly tale.

Humans and Cannibalism

Why would human beings become cannibals? In several societies throughout the world, human flesh was considered a form of food. Some people believed that eating the dead body of another person would give them the desirable qualities of that person. For example, if the dead person was brave, their flesh would provide bravery to whoever ate it. Head-hunting peoples ate the body parts or heads of their enemies to absorb their physical strength.

In some cultures, it was common for people to eat the body of a dead relative. This form of cannibalism, known as **endocannibalism**, was an act of respect—a way of preserving the dead person inside the bodies of the living relatives.

Traces of human cannibalism still exist in remote areas of the world.

In several cultures, cannibalism was part of selected religious practices and ceremonies. The Aztecs of southern Mexico, for example, conducted large-scale ceremonies in which thousands of war captives and other victims were sacrificed to their gods. The bodies of the victims were eaten to bring the Aztecs closer to their gods. In India, people belonging to a certain religious group would often eat the sick and aged members of their villages to please their goddess.

In a few cultures, people believed that cannibalism was the only way an enemy's spirit could be destroyed. If the body was consumed, the ghost would have nowhere to live. Both the body and the spirit were thus eliminated at the same time.

Today, people in developed countries don't eat other human beings. In very rare instances, however, starvation can force some people to resort to cannibalism. This occurred during the winter of 1846–1847 when the ill-fated Donner party was snowbound in the Sierra Nevada mountains of eastern California. And, in 1972, sixteen members of a soccer team survived for 70 days after their airplane crashed in the Andes mountains. How did they do it? You guessed it!

For the most part, however, we believe that cannibalism is both horrifying and wrong. As human beings, we are able to reason and act according to acceptable and established forms of behavior. The rules and laws made by the society in which we live have determined that cannibalism is wrong. In short, killing and eating other human beings is illegal, immoral, and improper. But animals have no such rules.

The Andes mountains, where an air crash made cannibalism necessary for human survival.

Survival and Cannibalism

Animals that have traits, characteristics, instincts, features, or behaviors that help them survive are able to reproduce. A new generation is born and the species goes on. Scientists refer to this as "the law of survival" or "the survival of the fittest." The new generation will carry those desirable traits or characteristics and will also produce offspring. So beneficial traits are passed on to a new generation, giving those offspring a better chance for survival.

As you have read in this book, cannibalism is one way some species have adapted to their environment. While we may not approve of it, cannibalism helps some animal species survive. Or, to look at it another way, some animals are here today because they kill and eat their own kind.

Glossary

aerating—supplying something—usually a living organism—with oxygen.

cannibalism—when an animal or animal species eats other members its own kind.

endocannibalism—a form of human cannibalism in which individuals eat the body of a dead relative.

evolution—the process in which organisms develop special characteristics that help them survive and reproduce.

exoskeleton—a hard covering on the outside of an animal (for example, lobsters and grasshoppers). All insects have exoskeletons.

exploitation—when a stronger animal makes use of a weaker member of its own species.

extinct—when a species no longer exists or is no longer active.

froth—a mass of milky-white bubbles produced by some animals.

gestation—the period between fertilization and birth (in humans this period is nine months).

hibernation—a resting state some animals enter during the winter months.

larva—the second stage in the development of some animals.

litter—the offspring produced at one time by an animal.

mantid—a group of predatory insects, such as the praying mantis. They have two pairs of walking legs and feed on live insects.

metamorphosis—the stages of development through which some animals pass as they become adults.

mucus—a slippery substance secreted by certain body glands as a protective liquid.

oviduct—one of the tubes in a female animal that transport and feed the eggs.

prey—an animal hunted and eaten by another animal.

pupa—the third stage in the development of some animals, especially insects.

spiderling—a baby spider.

uterus—the portion of the oviduct in which a fertilized egg develops—known as the **womb** in mammals.

venom—a poisonous liquid produced by an animal and transmitted by a bite or sting.

vertebra—one of the bones that form the spinal column.

To Find Out More

Books

Else, George. *Insects and Spiders*. New York: Time-Life Books, 1997.

Fredericks, Anthony D. *Clever Camouflagers*. Minnetonka, MN: NorthWord Press, 1997.

Exploring the Oceans. Golden, CO: Fulcrum Publishing, 1998.

Little, Jocelyn. *World's Strangest Animal Facts*. New York: Sterling Publishing, 1994.

Seidensticker, John and Susan Lumpkin. *Dangerous Animals*. New York: Time-Life Books, 1995.

Tomb, Howard. *Living Monsters: The World's Most Dangerous Animals*. New York: Simon and Schuster, 1990.

Videos

Bite of the Black Widow. (Catalog No. A51633). Washington, DC: National Geographic Society, 1994.

Nature's Newborn. (Catalog No. 10036). Anaheim, CA: Diamond Entertainment Corporation, 1995.

Predators of North America. (Catalog No. A51180). Washington, DC: National Geographic Society, 1981.

CD-ROMs

Discovering Endangered Wildlife (Lyriq International Corp., 1701 Highland Ave., Cheshire, CT 06410). IBM [Grades 6–8].

Microsoft Dangerous Creatures (Microsoft Corporation, One Microsoft Way, Redmond, WA 98052). IBM & Macintosh [Grades 4-12].

The San Diego Zoo Presents the Animals 2.0 (Mindscape, 60 Leveroni Ct., Novato, CA 94949). IBM & Macintosh [Grades 1–8].

Sharks (Discovery Communications, 7700 Wisconsin Blvd., Bethesda, MD 20814). Macintosh [Grades 3–12].

Organizations and Online Sites

Defenders of Wildlife
1101 14th Street NW, Suite 1400
Washington, DC 20005
http://www.defenders.org/index.html
This organization is dedicated to the protection of all native wild animals and plants in their natural environment.

National Audubon Society
666 Pennsylvania Avenue SE
Washington, DC 20003
http://www.audubon.com
This group focuses on research and education that helps protect and save threatened ecosystems.

National Wildlife Federation
1400 16th Street NW
Washington, DC 20036
http://www.nfw.org/
This organization works to promote environmental awareness and to help people conserve our natural resources.

Wildlife Conservation Society
185th St. and Southern Blvd.
Bronx, NY 10460
http://www.wcs.org/news
This group is dedicated to preserving biodiversity, teaching ecology, and inspiring care for all wildlife.

Young Entomologists' Society, Inc.
1915 Peggy Pl.
Lansing, MI 48910
http://insects.ummz.lsa.umich.edu/yes/yes.html
This organization provides young scientists with publications, programs, and information about all types of insects.

A Note on Sources

I first became interested in cannibal animals when I saw a program about them on the Discovery channel. I was fascinated by the different species of animals that practice this behavior, and I wanted to learn more. I searched on the Internet to gather detailed information about specific animals and species. Some of my favorite websites include those listed in "To Find Out More."

Next, I talked to reference librarians and children's librarians in several libraries in my area. They provided me with titles and resource materials to read. I also subscribe to about twelve different science and nature magazines. In addition, I read many nonfiction children's books by other authors such as Laurence Pringle, Seymour Simon, Gail Gibbons, Patricia Lauber, Sneed Collard, Donald Silver, and Ron Hirschi, to see what they have written about specific animals.

I am particularly indebted to Joseph Agro of AT&T and Eric Lund of the Rummler Brache Group who graciously provided me with valuable research and personal perspectives on cannibal animals. Additional thanks are extended to Dr. Kathy Carlstead at the National Zoo in Washington, DC, for her comments and suggestions during the revision process.

—*Anthony D. Fredericks*

Index

Numbers in *italics* indicate illustrations.

About the Author

Anthony D. Fredericks is nationally known for his energetic and highly practical presentations for strengthening elementary science instruction. His dynamic and stimulating seminars have captivated thousands of teachers from coast to coast.

His background includes extensive experience as a classroom teacher, author, professional storyteller, and university specialist in elementary science and language arts methods.

He has written more than forty books including the best-selling *The Complete Science Fair Handbook*, which he co-authored with Isaac Asimov. His children's books on animals and the environment have been highly praised by teachers and librarians across the country. He is currently a Professor of Education at York College in York, Pennsylvania.